TRUE NATURE

An Exploration Of Being Human

SHANNON COOPER

ISBN: 978-1-7750551-3-6

To all those bringing more love
and understanding to the world

"The field of the finite is all that we can see, hear, touch, remember, and describe. This field is basically that which is manifest, or tangible. The essential quality of the infinite, by contrast, is its subtlety, its intangibility. This quality is conveyed in the word 'spirit', whose root meaning is 'wind or breath.' This suggests an invisible but pervasive energy, to which the manifest world of the finite responds. This energy, or spirit, infuses all living things, and without it any organism must fall apart into its constituent elements. That which is truly alive in living systems is this energy of spirit, and this is never born and never dies."

- DAVID BOHM, THEORETICAL PHYSICIST

CONTENTS

FOREWORD

Whoever you are and however you managed to find yourself reading this book, might I just start by saying, I'm happy for you. You're about to embark on something equal parts subtle and gentle but also wildly profound and potentially life-altering. Cooper shares a simple understanding of the human experience and our place in the universe... both the universe of our minds and the universe that is all around us.

I don't typically like books like this. I either find them too intellectual or too new-age fluffy. But I almost instantly fell in love with this one. As I read her words, her elegant use of nature as metaphor for the human experience, and her transparent sharing of how learning about the infinite intelligence behind life freed her from her own anxieties I felt both relaxed and intrigued, intellectually stimulated and yet gently, soulfully carried.

I'll steal one of her brilliant lines, "Truth isn't true because of who said it or how it is said, it's true because of its nature." I feel the same about *True Nature*. It is an excellent book because of its truth and beauty. Not least of all because Cooper is a young writer writing elegantly about something both simple and complex. Mostly because what she writes is universally true and that truth will strike you at your core.

- Mara Gleason Olsen,
author of *One Thought Changes Everything*

INTRODUCTION

There are billions of stars in the sky. More than we can even fathom, let alone see. Sometimes we get lucky. We get a clear night where the universe opens up, we see a world that was previously invisible to us. Suddenly the big picture becomes apparent, we lose ourselves in the magic of bright lights dancing above us. We feel expansive, refreshed, connected, and in awe of the wonder of our world.

We know we can't always be seeing what we're seeing in that moment. We know come morning light the stars will disappear from our sight. Yet we also know next time the meteorological conditions allow, the view will present itself to us again. There's a comfort in that realization. We are soothed knowing that the stars are always there, even when we can't see them. We're at peace with the fact that night will melt into day but we know day will become night and there will again be opportunities to witness the beauty of a starry night. This is how glimpses of truth work: when you see them they're awe-inducing and world-expanding, yet even when you don't see them it's comforting to know that it exists just out of view.

You'll find it most helpful, in my experience, to read this book lightly without trying to 'figure it out'. Whenever our analytical minds are engaged, we often miss what's actually being said while we're busy trying to fit it into our existing worldview. All of that is completely natural, but we do ourselves a disservice by actively trying to take in information. Just let the words wash over you like waves on the beach, like listening to music or reading a message from a friend. Lightly and not too seriously.

I love metaphors because for the most part they allow us to gain a new perspective that eludes us when we're focused on the actual thing we're looking at. It allows our minds to open and expand in a way that is more creative and imaginative as opposed to analytical and systematic. Metaphors can loosen our thinking about life by helping us see something in a new way. I use them primarily because they have been immensely helpful to me in my journey of understanding what's true about life.

A metaphor can only go so far, and it's important to remember that what we're talking about is like it, but not actually it. While metaphors are helpful in trying to illustrate something we don't really have words for, the metaphor can only attempt to point to it. What is invisible is not easy to discuss. The very fact of using language to describe intangible forces or spiritual principles is inherently challenging. We'll just do our best not to take the words too seriously and try to get a feel for what's behind them.

Truth isn't true because of who said it or how it is said, it's true because of its nature. When something is simply true for everyone all the time, the evidence can be seen everywhere. Don't believe what you read just because you read it. Look for yourselves, test it out, see where it rings true for you. The beautiful thing about looking in the direction of truth is that you tend to find that it was always there, just waiting to be discovered.

WELCOME HOME

In the early 1970s on the small Canadian island of Salt Spring, an ordinary man named Sydney Banks had an enlightenment experience in which he glimpsed the fundamental principles at play behind our human experience. Although Syd saw it in a very clear, unifying way, the wisdom he was pointing to has been discussed by scholars, philosophers, mystics, religious leaders, thinkers, sages, writers, poets and many other seekers throughout the ages.

A principle is defined as 1) a fundamental source or basis for something and 2) a fundamental quality or attribute determining the nature of something. Syd did not create or invent the principles, they have been in operation since the beginning of time. He came to refer to these three principles as Universal Mind, Universal Consciousness and Universal Thought. In his book *The Missing Link*, Syd writes "Mind, Consciousness and Thought are the three principles that enable us to acknowledge and respond to existence. They are the basic building blocks." This psychological trinity forms the basic facts upon which everything else rests. Don't worry about getting it right away, just try to keep an open mind and it'll make more sense in the chapters to follow.

Universal Mind is the intelligent energy behind all of life. It's life supporting life; the power source behind everything and anything anyone can ever know. Syd taught that "the big Mind is the Divine Mind - the Universal Mind, which is the intelligence of literally all things in this world or any other world" and that "there is one Universal Mind, common to all, and wherever you are, it is always with you, always."

Mind is the most essential essence: the source of everything, the purest potential in the universe. There is nothing beyond, behind or before it. It has been called the unknown, the not yet created, the Universe, the divine, God, the quantum field, the great all-ness, the fertile void, the Tao, pure energy, the great nothingness, potentiality, the infinite, and more. No name can change its essence, call it what you wish.

Universal Consciousness is our capacity for awareness. It's what allows us to have an experience of life, it brings our thinking to life and creates sensory experience for each and every one of us. Syd wrote that "consciousness gives us the ability to realize the existence of life" and taught that "consciousness is infinite - there is no end to it."

Universal Thought is the force that creates our individual experience of reality. It is the colours that paint the picture of life. It is the vehicle between the form and the formless; the created and the not yet created. As Syd wrote "Thought is not reality; yet it is through Thought that our realities are created" and "you're only one thought away from happiness, you're only one thought away from sadness. The secret lies in Thought. It's the missing link everybody in this world is looking for."

Principles, by their very nature, are descriptions rather than prescriptions. Learning the principles is not like learning a technique, or a better set of actions to implement in your life. They don't prescribe actions, behaviours, techniques, tools, or how-tos which can be frustrating if that's what we think we need. Luckily, we don't. Try not to read this looking for the "how-to", just be open and curious about seeing something new.

The principles point to what's true about the human operating system: how it is that we come to have an experience of anything. They simply illuminate what is occurring on a deeper, more foundational level. They describe what is always at play behind the specific details of whatever is happening in our lives.

The periodic table of elements, for example, represents the core chemical building blocks that make up everything in the physical universe. The combinations may vary but there is nothing in the universe that is not composed of one or more of these basic elements. Similarly, the three principles of mind, consciousness and thought make up every experience that anyone has ever had, is currently having or can ever have. There is nothing outside of the scope of these principles. Every experience is a combination of these three elements, manifesting in whatever form they happen to be taking in any moment.

While these principles can be discussed intellectually it's only when we see them insightfully, literally a sight from within, that they effortlessly transform our relationship to our experience. Insight isn't something we can make happen, it's the natural result of when our minds settle down enough for something new to come through. I'm going to be pointing to the same thing, but in a variety of different ways which will hopefully give you a sense of the bigger picture, spark your curiosity and open you up to your own insights.

It may sound that I'm making the same point repeatedly, that's done intentionally. The point is simple yet sufficiently revolutionary that it's worth coming at it from different angles. Despite it being very simple it's not always easy to see. Don't worry if it doesn't make sense right away, we often get touched deeper than our intellect can comprehend at the time.

The power in 'getting it' is that once we really know how something works we can take it into account, factor it in and work with it rather than against it. If we don't know how something works we're likely to run on superstition, trying to remember what seemed to work last time and being puzzled when we get varying results. Rather than relying on luck, chance, or superstition, there's power in understanding how something really works. We waste less energy while tending to have better results.

What I find so unbelievably helpful about learning the principles is that it points to how things work for everyone, all the time, across the board. No exceptions; no exemptions. Looking to what is always true has the power to help us in all areas of our lives because we get reoriented to what's constant. As much as it looks like the outside world is causing us to feel a certain way, our feelings can only ever be caused by our thinking in the moment. The moment fresh thinking arrives it brings a new feeling since thinking and feeling are two sides of the same coin.

We can never be stuck in any experience because the nature of thought is fluid. We can't hold it in place no matter how hard we try because thought is ephemeral, there's simply no way to grip it in our minds. Even if we try to hold on to thought at some point we'll get distracted and naturally let go, which opens up space for new thought to rush in. The fact that the system only works one way gives us some comfort. Thought comes from the formless and returns to the formless without any effort on our part. We're not in charge of putting thoughts in or taking thoughts out of our minds.

There's so little we actually have to do. Yet when we misunderstand where our experience comes from, it looks like there's so much to do, so much to figure out and lots to work on. It's not our job to manage, control or change our thinking. Funnily enough we tend to get better thinking when we leave our thinking alone. The system seems to be beautifully designed to give us higher quality of thought when we're not trying to control what shows up.

Our mind self-corrects when we allow it to self-correct. Even when we hold onto a lot of thought it self-corrects eventually because that's how it's designed. The reason so many of us don't know this is not because it isn't true, it's simply because we rarely leave our thinking alone long enough or often enough to notice its self-correcting tendency. When we're not looking for something we tend not to find it, yet the moment we know where to look we'll naturally begin to see it more and more, because it has always been there.

One of the first insights I had while learning these principles is that I noticed just how often my mind cleared. I saw how often unhelpful thinking just left without me having to do anything. I realized how many times an hour I returned to a quiet mind, even if just for a moment. Every time I fell into this quiet state it felt like coming home. I found a sense of well-being, a sense of peace and calm that I started to realize was the default. Not a fluke, not an end result, not an achievement. This was the start of me seeing the truth about our innate health.

THE NATURE OF TRANSFORMATION

I want to talk just a bit about how change happens. We're told if we want to make change happen we need to have discipline, willpower, motivation, a list of the right tools and techniques, the right people, the right circumstances, good genetics, a little bit of luck and lots of hard work. Nothing could be further from the truth. Having been an anxious, stressed-out mess for most of my life I was utterly convinced that rediscovering my mental well-being and coming home to a place of peace was something that I needed to work very hard at.

The entire self-help industry is focused on giving you the right beliefs, ideas, tools, strategies, motivational quotes and techniques to show you how you can improve yourself and be a 'better you'. The best you, full of well-being, love, and peace, is and has always been underneath the layers of thinking that we mistake as truth. There's nothing you need to do, nowhere you need to get to. Everything you have ever wanted and needed is within you, by default, simply by virtue of being a spiritual being having a human experience.

I didn't know that at the time. Transforming my mental health looked and felt like something that was going to be really hard. So when I started learning about these principles, out of sheer philosophical curiosity and amusement, I didn't have any expectations that it was going to make my anxiety disappear, or help with my unhealthy eating habit, or make me more creative, or significantly lower my stress, or transform my relationships across the board. I didn't have anything 'on it'. I listened with an open mind and a curious heart because I thought it was philosophically fascinating, and I was getting really tired of reading self-help articles that weren't helping despite all the work I was doing.

So you can imagine my surprise when a few months later I realized that I hadn't felt anxious in a while. I didn't know it would last, so I kept it to myself while trying not to get my hopes up. It seemed impossible that years of suffering could fade away without my doing. Yet I couldn’t figure out what I was doing differently to account for the change. I cautiously waited a few more months for the chronic anxiety to return, certain that it couldn’t be that easy. To this day (it’s been a few years) it hasn’t come back.

Over time it's become clear to me that correcting the misunderstanding I had about how the mind works, seeing what’s true about my anxious feelings (it wasn’t what I was taught) and seeing how I was innocently messing with a self-correcting system completely and effortlessly transformed my mental health. Things looked and felt completely different even though my circumstances had changed very little, if at all. Huge problems suddenly looked like situations. Solutions started appearing out of nowhere. I started sleeping through the night. I haven't had a panic attack since. It didn’t happen overnight, it unfolded gradually over the course of many months. Yet today my day-to-day level of well-being, contentment and resilience is higher than I even thought possible.

I don't know what I would have missed if I had been looking to this understanding for a quick fix, a solution to uncomfortable feelings, or a way to never feel anxious again. What I really got was so much more than that. What before had looked so solid, scary, real and dangerous now looks more neutral, flexible, transient and safe.

This conversation has pointed me to an organic rediscovering of what has always been true and what we always have going for us. I'm grateful everyday that I was open-minded enough to stay curious, even when it went against everything I was taught about how the world works. If you allow your mind to be open, you just might feel that too.

WATER

FLOAT ON

"All we are is peace, love, and wisdom, and the power to create the illusion that we are not." - Jack Pransky

When we don't see that we are innately healthy, our well-being often feels conditional on external circumstances. Happiness can feel like our job, and one we're failing at most of the time. We're constantly inundated with prescriptions for feeling good: do this, say this, buy this, believe in this, eat this, drink this, be this kind of person and your life will be good, everyone will love you, you'll be so happy, healthy, beautiful and never have a bad day ever again. Yeah, right.

Gaining an understanding of the inside-out nature of our experience reminds us that we can only live in the feeling of our thinking, not in the feeling of the external world. Thoughts just show up randomly in our minds. They have no inherent meaning but for the meaning we give them. They aren't a reflection of reality existing independently of us, rather they're a projection of the reality we're creating within us moment by moment.

Consciousness is the principle that brings our thinking to life such that it looks real and appears to be coming from outside of us. Consciousness is often described as the best special effects department imaginable. Thought gets brought to life by consciousness so powerfully that it feels like it has to be coming from life. By thought I'm not talking about any specific thought, although that is certainly included. I'm talking about thought in a broader way. Sydney Banks described it as a vehicle through which the formless comes into form. Each and every sensation, electrical impulse, heartbeat, experience, emotion, memory, etc is all brought to us through this energy and made manifest in our awareness through consciousness.

Consciousness is incredibly seductive, it plays the movie of our minds out in our senses which tricks us into thinking that we're experiencing 'the real world': an independent reality that exists before our perception of it. That's not to say there isn't an outside world, there are certainly physical structures like our bodies, furniture, stars, galaxies, plants, animals and people. It's just that we can never have a direct experience of any of those things. All we can directly experience is thought, 100% of the time, no exceptions.

The problem isn't that we have thinking that suggests what a happy life should look like. The only problem, if there even is one, is that we take those thoughts seriously, believing them to be accurate data about what would really make us happy, instead of seeing the truth that they're just random ideas that showed up in our mind looking real. Without taking certain thoughts seriously they lose their power over us. This is because they never had any inherent power to begin with. Their power was a result of misunderstanding what they are, where they come from and why we have them.

We have brains that are incredibly analytical and computer-like, and so we will have thoughts about how life should be from birth until death. Seeing deeply that those suggestions are just random ideas, not an actual path containing important information about life, is what allows us to be free of them. When we see them for what they are they lose their control over us.

When my anxiety was really bad, I had no idea that the thoughts telling me what I needed to do, be, or have were simply random thought occurrences that I was taking seriously because I misunderstood them. I didn't know at the time that seeing a deeper truth about these thoughts would naturally change my relationship with them, such that even when they still show up, they don't get my energy or attention.

We are always fundamentally well, regardless of what we do or don't do, regardless of what we do or don't say, regardless of what we think or don't think. None of those things have the power to change our default setting of peace and well-being. Learning this felt like discovering I could float after a lifetime of trying to keep my head above water.

Up until a few years ago I believed I couldn't swim. I had failed swimming lessons as a child an embarrassing amount of times and was scared of deep water. During one particular heat wave I was on a beautiful island celebrating the wedding of two dear friends when I came down with heat stroke. The pacific ocean was the coldest source nearby so once the worst of the illness subsided I was coaxed into conquering my swimming fears. Fortunately I was in the presence of multiple trained lifeguards, so I reluctantly lowered myself off the side of the dock into the ocean with no sea floor in sight.

I had always hated treading water, I was never able to keep my head above water for more than a few seconds and it was always physically draining and emotionally terrifying. Observing what a colossal failure I was at treading water, a lifeguard friend suggested I just take a deep breathe, tip backwards and float.

You see, I obviously knew intellectually that human bodies float; this wasn't headline news. But because I had never calmly floated on water that I couldn't stand up in, I believed that I couldn't do it. I didn’t actually know why, I just knew I had failed at staying afloat every time I tried. So imagine my surprise when I took a deep breath, kicked my legs out in front of me, and just relaxed on the surface of the ocean.

Turns out, I can float. It was incredible. It felt so freeing and was so comforting to my heat-ravaged body to float in cool water. The irony is that once I discovered I could float treading water became much easier. Knowing that I could default into floating when I was struggling to keep my head above water made the treading water movements way more relaxed, fluid, and easy. It took away all the tightness and thrashing that I was used to when I was just desperate not to drown.

Realizing the principles behind the human experience is the equivalent of learning we float: we have always floated and we will always continue to float. When we discover that we our innate health and well-being is unconditional, it suddenly doesn’t make sense for us to thrash about chasing outside circumstances as a path to fulfilment. We can just kind of float through life, doing what it occurs to us to do in the moment, and savouring the joy of the moment. What we’re looking for is already within, our wellness never leaves us regardless of what we happen to be experiencing in the moment.

Instead of needing to check all the boxes for the perfect life, we start to realize that our experience of life doesn't come from outside circumstances. If it did work that way we would be insulated from feeling sad, angry, stressed or fearful once we got the partner, job, house and friends we wanted. Life doesn't work like that. Our feelings can't come from other people or circumstances, no matter how much it seems like it does.

We don't need to struggle to keep our head above water, or exhaust ourselves swimming to certain targets. We can take a deep breath, look to where our experience truly originates, and discover that floating is our nature. It's how we're designed. We've always had this capacity, we just tend to have a lot of conditioned thinking that tells us otherwise.

The only thing that can take us away from our inherent peace of mind is falling for the illusion that our well-being is something we have to obtain. In a quiet mind we reconnect with the good feelings we're searching for. When the level of thought interference is low, we feel it quite naturally and effortlessly; when there's lots of interference, not so much. We're always able to just float, buoyed by our innate well-being as we go through life.

THE ENDLESS RIVER

"Out beyond the ideas of wrongdoing and rightdoing, there is a field. I'll meet you there. When the soul lies down in that grass the world is too full to talk about. Ideas, language, even the phrase 'each other' doesn't make any sense." – Rumi

The flow of thought operates like a river. Rivers flow continuously as the nature of water is to move from higher elevations to lower elevations across landscapes. They can flow slowly or quickly but they're constantly in movement, even with a frozen surface there's still movement underneath.

The energy of thought is constantly moving, it flows through us continuously without any effort on our part. Where we tend to get stuck is we focus on a specific bit of what's flowing in front of us and miss the river as a whole. We do the mental equivalent of scooping up a bucket of water. We look at the details of what's in the bucket, the bits of debris, leaves or twigs that just happened to be flowing by at the time. We may think something has to be done about the debris as we try to pick out the leaves one by one.

Things are always going to show up in the river, but they don't mean anything about the river. We often miss the fact that the leaves will keep flowing by if we don't stop them. Our experience is constantly changing, feelings arise and disappear in a matter of seconds. Yet when something comes up that we don't like, we scoop out the flowing water to analyze what's in the bucket and generalize our observations to the whole. We conclude from analyzing some anxious thoughts that we must be an anxious person. We miss all the times we're not anxious. We miss all the times that our minds are clear with a natural relaxed flow.

The danger of looking to a single experience, a single bucket, is that we miss the larger whole. Our big picture view gets lost in the details of the moment. We miss the fact that if we had just allowed the leaves to flow downstream we would get something new in the next moment. Sometimes the bucket will be completely clear water with no debris. Sometimes it will be full of leaves. We could scoop dozens of buckets and see that they are clear, leafy or full of debris and it still wouldn't mean anything about the nature of the river.

The nature of the river is renewal, always something upstream that hasn't flowed in yet. This is why there's so much hope for anyone. Whether it's depression, stress, loss, heartbreak or trauma, we're not stuck in anything permanently. We mistake our temporal experiences for truth about who we are. This simply isn't true.

We can't know anything fundamental about the river by looking at what happened to be floating in it at any moment in time. We can only know the nature of the river by looking at what doesn't change. Looking upstream to the continuous flow of movement, the fact that water is always there but never stagnant. Filling up buckets, analyzing their content and making generalizations just looks like a less helpful way to understand the river.

Getting unstuck is as simple as looking around us to the natural flow of life. The movement of change and renewal is always working on our behalf. As long as we're open to fresh thinking and a new experience of life, there's nothing stopping it.

PEACE OF MIND

Our minds are naturally calm. We're all familiar with the feeling of a quiet mind, a beautiful feeling, or a simple moment of relaxation. That peace of mind is the default that always exists beneath our thinking. Whenever we're not feeling well it's simply that we're caught up in thought. Our thinking creates internal movies that trick us into believing what we think about life is how it is.

The space of love, well-being and wisdom isn't the end result of achievement, success or ideal external circumstances, no matter how much we've been taught that's how it works. Well-being is the state humans rest in; what's always there and what's felt whenever our thinking quiets down.

I was fortunate enough to spend a lot of my childhood camping all over my home of British Columbia, Canada. Lakes have captured my heart ever since I was young. In its default state, the surface of a lake is perfectly still. Especially around sunset when the day is winding down, lakes often look like liquid glass holding the reflection of the sky.

At any time something could fall into the water, wind could pick up, or rain could start. But what happens on the surface can't touch the deepest part underneath. The deeper you go the more pure and quiet it gets. The deepest parts are untouched by the surface fluctuations. Regardless of what experience we have, it can't touch the deepest part of us.

Peace of mind is the default setting for everyone, all the time, no exceptions. We'll all experience wind storms from time to time. They can look like worried, anxious, fearful, panicked, fast, or busy thinking. We'll all have rain storms in our minds, manifesting as low moods, depressed thinking, insecurities, grief, loss, disappointment and failure. We experience the whole gamut of human experience, from the most enjoyable to the least enjoyable.

It's helpful to know that humans all work the same way. We're all up against the same things, and we all have the same things going for us. We're all up against unrecognized thought and the seduction of consciousness. Sometimes our life is going to look chaotic, difficult and frightening. That's okay because what we all have going for us is that we are inherently calm, effortlessly loving and naturally peaceful by default.

What happens on the surface is just what happens on the surface. We may or may not enjoy it while it's happening but that's okay. It can't touch the deepest part of us, it can't last forever (such is the nature of any storm, including thought storms) and when the storm clears out we find ourselves just as peaceful as before.

LET IT BE

Understanding the nature of thought can open the door to glimpsing the illusory nature of life. Because what we think is what we see, life tends to unfold like a self-fulfiling prophecy. All the reasons, evidence and justification we have for why something really is a problem independent of our thinking about it, are also thought-created. We're the judge, the jury and the defendant all in one. We can find evidence to support any thought because the very thing that makes those ideas real to us is the fact that they get brought to life by consciousness.

We're always living in a sea of fluid thought: it's everything we touch, taste, hear, see and smcll. Occasionally in our sea of thought we bump up against icebergs: things that appear in our way that appear solid, substantial and real. If we don't know that icebergs are made of water, that they form out of water and dissolve back into water, we'll naturally treat them like the exception to the rule. We then start brainstorming how to get rid of these solid icebergs. We think we need tools such as shovels and pickaxes.

The icebergs certainly appear more real, substantial or fixed than the water they're floating in, but in truth they're made of the exact same thing, albeit in different forms. The form is temporary. Once the ice melts it will return back to the sea. We believe that we have to chip away at the ice in an attempt to get rid of it. We don't see that the iceberg will just resolve itself if we warm up the water a bit and give it time.

There's nothing that we need to do; natural processes tend to operate better without our input. Water forms into ice and ice forms into water naturally, completely without our control or interference. Believe it or not our mental icebergs work the same way.

Whenever we label or diagnose our experience as a problem, we're treating one thought-created experience as different from the rest of our thought-created experience. It's the same as mistaking the different forms water can take. The iceberg may be habitual or conditioned thinking, yet it's still made of thought.

We call our icebergs anxiety, depression, anger problem, phobias, failure, heartbreak or any number of labels. Yet we miss the fact that if those experiences weren't treated differently, they wouldn't be such a problem. We all fall into the trap of thinking our issue is special, different or unique. But when we do this it tends to make that thing seem more solid, substantial and real than the rest of what flows through our awareness.

Those experiences don't feel as fluid because we treat them as though they're ice, not water. We employ strategies, tools and techniques to try to chip away at it instead of raising the water temperature (aka level of understanding) and letting it just melt away.

In time the sun and the flow of currents will naturally melt the iceberg into liquid water. This is how problems resolve themselves overnight. It's how an event can feel so terrible and unmanageable one moment and a week later the obvious thing has been done and it's taken care of. This is the innate resiliency of the human system, thought is always changing and our lives change with it. There seems to be a kindness to the design that grants us new perspective, making it so that we don't have to do anything about the bulk of our problems; with time they'll resolve themselves or the solution will become obvious.

Experience comes and goes. Thought comes and goes. We feel it until we don't, then we feel something else. This process is happening all the time, whether we are aware of it or not. Change is a natural process, it's not something we need to make happen, despite what we've been raised to believe.

We've been socially conditioned to focus on the content of thoughts to the detriment of realizing the fact of thought. The fact is what we're feeling in each and every moment comes from our thinking and will change the moment our thinking does. We don't have to wait for our external circumstances to change in order to feel better. We're not at the mercy of feeling bad because of who holds political office, what tone of voice our partner used with us or what the weather's doing. The details don't matter once we start to wake up to the fact that we're feeling off because our thinking is off in the moment. That's all. End of story.

All experience is made of the same stuff, comes from the same source and shares the same nature. There's freedom to be found in that. If we don't like how life looks to us, just give the ice a chance to melt. If we don't like how we're feeling, give the ice a chance to melt. If we feel like something is a huge problem, give the ice a chance to melt. Mental icebergs tend to dissolve a lot quicker than actual icebergs. All of our icebergs simply have yet to dissolve back into the sea, that's okay, in time they will.

GO WITH THE FLOW

"You are not a drop in the ocean. You are the entire ocean in a drop." – Rumi

Thought and feeling come through us like waves on a shore. An ocean wave forms and then returns to the ocean, ready for the next wave to take form. Every thought/feeling wave we've ever had has come through our system, created a full sensory experience and then returned from whence it came. This is why we're not stuck in the same feelings we felt as kids. I'm sure I'm not the only one who's had a moment where I truly believed that I would be stuck in a feeling forever, but time has proved that's simply not possible.

Thought is always moving, always changing and always flowing, even when it's not different enough to catch our attention. Our brains are really efficient machines which tend to categorize similar feelings into one mood. So even when we're in a bad mood, we're still having hundreds of different thoughts all with their corresponding feelings.

But once we've labelled it as 'bad day' we notice all the thoughts and feelings that support that, while ignoring or dismissing the outliers. The subtle nuances tend to get blurred together by the lens of how we're seeing life in the moment.

The ocean of thought keeps making waves: temporary forms that crash on the shore, give us an experience, and leave. They're random, unpredictable and impersonal. Even on our worst days, days full of panic attacks, crippling not-leaving-my-bed depression, tough illness, or unexpected injury, there's still variance from one moment to the next. There's still flow, even if it's not to the degree that we wish.

Even when it goes unnoticed, even when we label it away, there is still thousands of times a day where the energy of thought comes through us like waves on a beach. It begins in the formless, takes a form, gives us the ensuing experience, and returns to the formless to make way for the next wave of experience. This dance of energy is a universal constant, we don't know what will show up next but we know something will. The content can be anything we could ever imagine, as it's fully creative, pure potential.

Yet whether the next wave is an anxious sensation, a surprised reaction, a joyous thought, tears of gratitude, a pang of hunger, nostalgia, despair or absolute enchantment, anything and everything comes to us as waves from this eternal ocean. The same energy that powers the tides, waves and ocean currents of physical bodies of water also powers our human experience. The details are always changing yet the underlying principle is a constant. I find it so comforting to know that we have infinite waves ahead of us bringing us fresh thinking and new feeling, ultimately recreating our lives from the inside-out.

AIR

BREATH OF LIFE

In each and every moment we're being breathed automatically, yet we're not the ones doing it. We don't have to put in the effort, remember it or otherwise make it happen. Yet when it comes to our minds we're taught it's our job to figure everything out. Thinking, like breathing, is a passive process that we can become temporarily involved in. We can actively inhale or exhale, just as we can consciously think a specific thought but we're not responsible for putting thoughts in our minds any more than we're responsible for putting breath in our lungs.

It's not even our job to change the thinking that does show up. We don't have to monitor our thoughts. When we stop analyzing, trying to figure things out or otherwise meddling in our thinking, the system is free to work as designed: clear, easy and effortlessly.

When we leave our thinking alone we create space in our minds to see something new about life. We can start to see that our thinking is operated by something bigger than us, something that's universal because we all work the same way. The same energy that takes care of our breathing also takes care of our psychological functioning. We don't have to do anything to get fresh thinking or fluidity of experience, they're gifts.

Sure, in the short-term we can make ourselves breathe and make ourselves think, but we don't have to do either of them, they're being done for us automatically. The less we interfere with the system the better it operates. When we don't hold our breath new breath rushes in, just as when we don't hold onto thought new thought rushes in. There's nothing we have to do to bring in another breath other than let go of the current one; our experience works the same way. From birth to death new breath and new thought will come to us effortlessly.

As soon as there's space for new thinking to show up it does. We're all made of the energy of Mind and this intelligence knows how to take care of all of what it creates. Our physical systems of breathing, digestion, circulation, healing injuries and maintaining homeostasis are run on our behalf. Our input or know-how is not necessary. Our mind is no different, it will operate consistently without us doing anything.

Imagine how exhausting it would be to have to consciously and constantly breathe every breath. Most of us can see how silly that is, yet we treat our mind as if it's our business. The positive thinking movement sounds nice in theory, but it perpetuates the misunderstanding of our mind. It encourages us to police our thinking; analyzing, sorting and changing 'negative' thinking into 'positive' thinking. My first and only university psychology class was Positive Psychology and the homework exercises were exhausting, unhelpful and counterproductive.

It's impossible to do away with negative thinking, we simply weren't designed to have pink fluffy lives. Somehow this idea got passed around that life should be great and we should be happy all the time. Which just makes us feel worse when we can't get rid of our negative feelings. There is nothing we need to do to change how we're feeling. There is nothing we should do to change how we're feeling.

If we don't like how we're feeling we can realize it's coming from thought in the moment and allow the mind to self-correct. We weren't designed to have control over our thoughts. I actually used to think it was a problem that I couldn't control my thinking, now I see that it's part of the beauty of the design: we were never meant to do it which is why it's impossible to actually pull off.

The beauty and simplicity of this understanding is that we see we don't have to manage anything in order to have a rich experience of life. When we get out of our own way, the magnificence of life is naturally revealed to us. Whenever we are actively using our minds to try to change our experience we're just making it harder than it needs to be.

We can use our breath deliberately in yoga practice just as we can use our gift of thought to work on complex mathematical equations, but when it comes to moving through life with grace we do better the less we get in the way. Analyzing problems just adds a lot of extra noise to the system. Like too much static it interferes with the signal of wisdom. There is absolutely a time and place for a logical reasoning approach, but it won't help us when we need clarity, compassion or guidance. Just by allowing ourselves to be psychologically lived, our lives will naturally get 'figured out' without us having to make that our job.

THE GREAT GIG IN THE SKY

"Why, then, 'tis none to you, for there is nothing either good or bad, but thinking makes it so. To me it is a prison. Well, then it isn't one to you, since nothing is really good or bad in itself— it's all what a person thinks about it" - William Shakespeare

The northern lights are a beautiful natural phenomenon. Swirling energy of different colours dancing on the dark background of the night sky. The aurora borealis is flowing energy manifesting in different shapes and colours moment by moment. Sometimes it appears as long strings of green light, sometimes circles of blue or spirals of purple, yet it's all just temporary forms of the same energy.

Since we can only experience life through the power of thought in the moment, if we gathered a hundred people to watch the light show each person would have a different experience. Some would likely be mesmerized, some would rather be elsewhere, some would be distracted, some would have opinions about which manifestations are best, some would only like certain colours, shapes, or patterns… the possibilities are endless.

Electrically charged particles collide with oxygen and nitrogen in the atmosphere, and we have preferences, judgements, observations and opinions based on whatever we happen to be thinking. We all will have a different experience of the same physical event in the outside world because the experience of that moment is being brought to us by our own minds, not by the lights themselves.

This is true of life across the board. It's the reason why I can listen to a song and fall head over heels in love while it's irritating to someone else, and vice versa. It explains the entire diversity of human preferences, why we like different foods and agree with different political views. Like Shakespeare realized centuries ago, it's not the thing itself but rather the thinking that makes it so. We like what we like, dislike what we dislike and are neutral about things entirely based on our thinking about them. Which is actually incredibly hopeful since thinking changes faster and easier than circumstances. New thought is what enables shifts to take place, everything from someone getting comfortable with feelings of grief to solving complex global issues. Regardless of the scale, new thought is the missing ingredient.

We can only ever live in our own thought-created reality, never in the reality of the world. Mind, consciousness, and thought are the only things with the power to create experience for us. When we don't see where our experience of life comes from it's easy to mistake our muddled thinking for a real-life problem. A 'real life problem' makes us powerless victims, doomed to be at the mercy of things beyond our control. A thought-created problem means we're only stuck insofar as we buy into that illusion. When we see something different we feel something different and life is different, even if nothing outside of us has changed.

Things themselves are neutral. Purple lights in the night sky aren't any more beautiful than green lights, despite my opinion. My favourite bands aren't objectively the best artists out there, they're just what I happen to love to listen to at this time in my life. I love mangoes and avocados but I understand that just because I love them does not make them the best fruit. I can think, believe and prefer anything, that's not the problem. I only lose my way when I falsely believe that because I think something, I must be right. I'm right only in my mind, not as an objective fact of life.

My thinking is what brings me my feelings about those things, not the artists, fruits or northern lights themselves. What we think, like, believe and do is completely up for grabs since it's not caused by an independent reality outside of our own minds. None of our thinking is inherently true because we're only ever experiencing our mind, not the thing itself. We can think anything about anything, and we don't have to think anything about anything. The freedom is all ours.

EMPTY SPACES

"The soul has been given its own ears to hear things the mind does not understand." - Rumi

Appearances can be incredibly deceiving. We often get ourselves into trouble when we take what we see at face value: it looks that way therefore it is that way. Quantum physicists discovered there's a large amount of empty space in what appears to be solid matter. In addition to subatomic particles, solid matter is comprised mostly of formless energy.

Just consider that for a second. If the entire physical world is made of energy appearing solid, then it's no wonder that formless principles such as mind, consciousness and thought are going to elude us most of the time. They're powerful yet invisible. It really is no surprise that we continue to fall for the illusion that we're perceiving the outside world as it is. It doesn't look to us that we're projecting our thinking onto the world of form, yet that's what's always going on.

We can't trust that things are how they appear. We can't trust that our perceptions are accurate data of what is real beyond our senses. Our senses deceive us. A straight stick looks bent in a glass of water but it's just a trick of the light. That's all well and good if we know it's an illusion.

When we understand that light waves operate differently in water than in air we can take that into account and therefore won't get tripped up as easily. When we don't understand how that works, it can be confusing, troubling or downright frightening. When we fail to account for the fact that our perceptions – how life looks to us – is always changing moment to moment, we innocently believe what we see is how it is. We start to believe that our way is the way; that we're seeing life accurately. That's how it really looks and feels!

But our senses can't tell us how life is, independent of us. Our senses are informed by the principles of mind, thought and consciousness. They're not informed by the world. Our experience is internally generated moment by moment through the unfolding of these principles. It can look like we're the victim of someone else's behaviour or unfair circumstances. It can look like life happens to us, but it can only ever happen through us.

A simple example of this is when we're waiting on a text from a friend. Our minds can make up a million reasons why we haven't heard from them, and we can become convinced they're mad at us, trying to spite us, or dead. But then we get a text saying they were on a camping trip out of cell service and suddenly the story we made up is revealed as just that: a story we made up. We feel silly for taking it personally and believing the worst-case scenario. We see how we took the neutral situation of not hearing from someone to mean something about the state of our relationship with them.

This is why insightful understanding is so powerful. Intellectual understanding happens when we try to make rational sense of something, whereas seeing something insightfully is realizing that life is not what it appears to be. This glimpse of the cosmic joke of the universe opens us up to understanding a deeper truth about life: that we see whatever we think but that doesn't make it so. When we really understand that things are not as they appear, it opens the door to see more about what is true for everyone, always.

DREAMS

"Life is a divine dream suspended between the boundaries of time, space and matter" - Sydney Banks

I find it fascinating to reflect on the fact that the same system that gives us daytime thought is what gives us night-time thought in the form of dreams. When we're awake we tend to take our thinking seriously, whereas when we're asleep we see the inherent randomness and meaninglessness of it all. This is why I love the term day-mare because it reminds me that the same system that creates stories at night is what creates the story of our lives by day. Our imagination is always at play, it's just easier to see that when we're lying in bed with our eyes closed.

It's easy to see dreams as an illusion, mirage, or arbitrary set of ideas that flow through our mind in any given moment. Yet it's often harder to see that that's also true of our daytime thought. The principle of thought does not selectively operate based on the time of day. It does not create dreams any differently than daydreams. The difference is the relationship we have to that thinking. We're so used to thinking it works outside-in that we assume our daytime thought is coming from things in the world.

Thought gets brought to life by consciousness for everyone, all the time, no exceptions. It's behind every hallucination, daydream, lucid dream, night dream or perception. Seeing the arbitrary nature of thought is powerful because it highlights the disconnect between our experience of life and what's truly occurring in the world of form in any given moment. We think they're one and the same: what's going on in the world of form is our experience. It's not true.

I used to suffer a lot from hypochondriac thinking. I was always concerned that I was much sicker than I actually was, that my migraines were brain tumours, my coughs were lung infections and my lethargy must be chronic fatigue syndrome. I was utterly convinced that my symptoms were telling me that something was terribly wrong with me. What helped was the realization that the same physical symptoms didn't always produce the same experience in me.

My experience ranged anywhere from barely noticing it to full blown panic. Whether I took my symptoms as evidence that something was seriously wrong or whether I brushed them off, explained them away or otherwise waited them out, I was having radically different experiences of the same physical sensation. Sometimes it felt like a living nightmare, other times just an unpleasant experience and other times it was nothing. If my lethargy truly was a sign from the universe that I was chronically ill it wouldn't make sense that some days I wasn't bothered by it.

We're having an experience of thought: always and only. It's why sometimes we really notice something and get bothered by it and other times are completely oblivious to it. The physical sensation isn't determining our experience, our moment by moment thinking and level of consciousness is the sole determinant.

It's so much easier not to take our thinking seriously when we see that we're all just living in a waking dream. The creative capacity of thought is what allows us to experience all of our stories, whether they be nightmares, daymares or just habitual thought. We can be more suspicious of what we take as truth. No matter how compelling the story, once we see it as just a fictitious story we're free.

OBSCURED BY CLOUDS

"You are the sky. Everything else – it's just the weather."
- Pema Chödrön

Ultimately, this understanding has made me realize that we are the space in which experience arises, not the experiences themselves. This metaphor is probably the most popular one, and it's not exclusive to the principles, but I think it illustrates so beautifully what is at the heart of this conversation.

We are the sky. The nature of the sky is clear, vast, open, and bright. Weather shows up in that space, constantly moving and changing, always forming and reforming. We don't control the weather, nor are we passive victims of it. Weather does not affect the sky in any lasting way, no matter how violent the storm it never has the power to destroy the sun.

The weather doesn't mean anything about the sky; the sky is the constant backdrop to whatever manifestation of universal energy happens to show up in the moment. The weather operates in alignment with the fundamental principles of the physical world such as gravity, electromagnetism and the laws of thermodynamics. The details of the future weather remains a mystery. We know which forces will be behind the unfolding but not what the manifestation will be. In the same way our future experience is a mystery. We can think anything in any moment, we're not locked into the same habitual thinking we've had up until this point.

Our human experience operates much like the weather: it just shows up, is constantly moving and changing, is always forming and reforming, isn't controlled by us, can't affect us in any lasting way, can't ever destroy our well-being, doesn't mean anything, is a transient manifestation of universal energy and is operating in alignment with the fundamental principles of mind, consciousness and thought.

Our true nature is a bright, sunny day. That's not to say that we won't have weather systems come through, temporarily blocking the light of the sun and making our lives seem cold, dark, dreary and difficult. But then it clears out and reveals what was always there. We can get tricked by the clouds blocking the light, or get concerned when we don't feel that familiar warmth. Yet the sun is always there. Our well-being can't go anywhere. Our innate health can't go anywhere. Our wisdom can't go anywhere. Love can't go anywhere. We are made of universal energy, even when we can't feel it. As soon as the temporary weather of thought clears out, we're right back to love, peace, wisdom and well-being.

There's an old saying 'this too shall pass'. When I was working hard to fix myself and my anxiety, I would repeat this saying but I never understood the depth of it. I didn't see that it was pointing to something that's intrinsically true. Despite that I found it comforting because I realized that every experience I've ever had has passed, even if it took longer than I hoped it would. Now that I see more about how human beings operate, I see that statement as a reminder of what is true for everyone all the time, and less as a personal comfort. Anything and everything we can ever experience is the weather. We are always eternally the clear sky on a sunny day and there's nothing we need to do to make that true.

FIRE

ELECTRICITY

"When I am silent, I fall into that place where everything is music"
-Rumi

Universal mind is the power behind everything in the universe. It's like the electricity that we're always plugged into, it's with us everywhere we go. We're all born with the necessary systems to sustain life. Our circulatory system, respiratory system, digestive system and entire body is powered by this same energy.

This isn't a personal thing, it's a human being thing. This electricity is the buzz of our pulse, the heat of our body, what we have from the moment we're born until the moment we die. All the firing neurons in our brains, electrical impulses in our body, and movement of our muscles are forms that this energy takes in us to keep us alive.

Most of us have a sense that the biochemical operations of our bodies are run on our behalf. Yet when it comes to our psychological functioning, we often fail to see that that too is being done for us. It looks like our psychology benefits from our constant input and interference. We don't see that the mind has a mind of its own and runs like our other self-regulating systems. We can just let go and let it do its thing, without our meddling.

Our minds are run and regulated by the same energy that beats our heart. Regardless of the content of our psychology, how the system works is a constant. All of the greatest discoveries in human history, whether it be Einstein's theory of relativity, Copernican heliocentrism or even the discovery of electricity itself, came to a reflective mind without them having to do anything to make that happen. The energy behind life that we're all connected to is what allowed those realizations to come to mind.

In this way we are more like conduits, vessels or instruments for the energy of life to express itself through us. Creativity is a perfect example of this; we are creative beings by nature. This is incredibly obvious when we look at young children. Before they are 'taught' how to create they are natural creators, using their skills, imagination and sense of wonder to bring things to life. Creativity doesn't come from intellectual education. It seems to be just built into the human design, capable of being expressed in many different ways. Becoming masters at a craft surely requires practice but the capacity for new ideas, connections and insights are the natural result of having minds that are powered by the intelligence of all things.

This intelligence shows up in countless ways in our everyday lives. Everything from a name popping into our head, to a lightbulb moment, to a stroke of inspiration. It can happen in the smallest ways such as a hunch about what's next, or it can completely revolutionize how humanity understands the laws of physics, mathematical theorems, or exploratory space missions. It's the source behind every new idea, perfect quote, masterpiece of art, beautiful music, intricate sculpture, timeless literature, breathtaking poetry, or jaw dropping cinema. It's the power source behind everything. Everything we've ever fallen in love with all originated from this universal energy coming through someone and into the world. If all seven billion of us knew we had this creative power, who knows what brilliance will get brought into the world next?

HELLO, GOODBYE

As a culture we're conditioned to spend so much time working on our experience of life. We pay so much attention to familiar, old, habitual thought. Unable to resist the siren song of our thinking, we often seek to analyze, discover, fix or change what we think. We make what has shown up in our minds very much about us. We treat it super personally.

The whole self-help movement is committed to making us aware of the content of our thinking so that we can actively create better thinking in the future, or reframe past thinking in a positive light. Not only is this exhausting, difficult and ineffective, it perpetuates the misunderstanding of what thought is. It makes it out to be something it's not and convinces people that negative thinking is bad and needs to be eliminated.

Instead of pointing us towards how fluid, impersonal and random the content of our thinking is, self-help asks us to really examine what's going on in our heads. Once we know what our problems are, we then need to put in time and effort to 'fix it', all while completely missing the fact that what we think isn't meaningful. Having a lot of information about the content of our thinking is not nearly as helpful as waking up to the fact that we are thinking creatures.

We can think of thought as raw dough, the unprocessed material of experience, out of which all baked creations arise. Consciousness would then be like the oven that brings this dough to life as bread so we can have an experience of that bread, it'll have a touch, taste, sight, smell, and sound. There's an infinite conveyor belt of raw dough going in one end, taking a form, getting baked in the oven, and coming out as bread.

As any baker will tell you, not all batches turn out perfectly every time. Not everything that comes out of the oven is fresh, mouthwatering, perfectly balanced deliciousness. Sometimes the recipe goes wonky, it stays in the oven too long or doesn't get cooked properly. Yet even when the end creation goes awry, the process still operates according to the same basic principles: raw dough in one end, the oven brings it to life, and then there's bread. The good news is that there's always new bread being baked right behind the failed loaf.

It doesn't do us any good to pay attention to each individual loaf of bread. If the bread gets burnt, was made with stale dough, or had some unfavourable additives, the most inefficient use of our energy would be to try to change that loaf by adding salt, sugar, butter, or scraping off the burnt bits. It's so much easier to just toss it, let it dissolve away, and look to the fresh creations coming out of the oven. It just won't make sense to get so engaged with our old stale thinking once we realize that delicious fresh thinking is on its way.

That's not to say that every loaf after it is going to be perfect, there will be as much variance in the loaves as there is in nature, a mysterious unpredictability that's kind of cool once we see how safe it really is. Once we realize that failed loaves are just failed loaves, we don't have to do anything with them. We don't have to change them. We don't have to eat them. We can just wait for fresh bread: the fresh, delicious, beautifully cooked loaves that are being created in the next moment.

In my own life I've seen this realization help with difficult problems. When something looks really problematic I have a sense there's something I'm just not seeing, the solution is just out of reach. When I'm preoccupied with buttering the burnt loaves of all my problems, I've simply forgotten how good fresh loaves taste. But when it inevitably appears it is so much better, more nourishing and satisfying than expected. No amount of wonky loaves can ever be as good as a fresh loaf, they're simply of a different kind and quality.

There's comfort that no matter how awful an experience is, it's a temporary form whose dissolution requires absolutely nothing from us. We're free to live our lives enjoying the delicious bread while leaving the wonky loaves alone. Just because they're baked in our kitchen doesn't mean we have to eat them until we're stuffed.

PLAY WITH FIRE

"It is the mark of an educated mind to be able to entertain a thought without accepting it." - Aristotle

When a thought forms in our head and we do absolutely nothing with it, it leaves within seconds. It's estimated we have between 60,000 and 100,000 thoughts per day. We don't remember most of them because we just let them flow through us unencumbered. Yet because we don't really see and understand the arbitrariness of thought, and since it looks like it's coming from the external world of people, events and circumstances, we have attachments to some of our thoughts.

This is especially evident when people have labels, diagnoses, habits, or addictions. They've been told by well-meaning professionals, society, or themselves that they're a certain type of person based on generalizable patterns in their behaviour. This identification with their label innocently puts a lot of focus and attention on specific thoughts, feelings, and behaviours. When I was experiencing a lot of anxiety, I was told (and thus believed) that I was an 'anxious person'. Pretty soon I became hypersensitive to any thoughts, feelings or behaviours of the anxious variety. So in my everyday living anxious feelings got a lot of attention while calm feelings got very little attention.

When we do this we become hypervigilant of certain thoughts. We innocently put fuel on the very fire we're trying to extinguish. Each thought is similar to a spark. It's a blip of energy taking a temporary form before extinguishing. The reason we don't experience all of our thoughts as sparks is because we add fuel to certain ones. We toss on logs of judgement, attachment, identity, fear, resistance, unease and with each log the little spark starts to look more like a fire. A spark being fed fuel and being fanned with energy and attention will quickly grow a lot larger.

In our misunderstanding we see the fire and take it as proof that it is something bigger than thought, that it is something 'out there' in life that we were right to be concerned about. It becomes a self-fulfiling prophecy. We innocently turn something small into a big deal and then look at the big deal and think "wow, see what a big deal this is!"

Please know that this is innocent. We're all doing the best we can in every moment and when we do this, it's okay. I suffered from anxiety for years and even though I was making it much worse than it needed to be, I didn't know that's what I was doing. I didn't know I was doing more harm than good because I lacked understanding. I had no clue that thought energy was what was actually creating my anxious thoughts and feelings.

Once I really got that I could still have anxious thinking, and it would feel unpleasant, but that all I was experiencing was temporary energy passing through my system, it just didn't seem like a good idea to fan the flames. I could still do it because we all have some free will, but the less it made sense to keep the fire going, the less I found myself doing it. We always do what makes sense for us to do in the moment. When a different action makes sense, we naturally act differently.

We're all capable of letting an experience pass through us without showering it with energy, attention and meaning. We do it all the time with thoughts that don't matter to us. We also have the power to give any thought meaning. We can make anything mean something, and make something mean anything if we so choose. It will appear real to us in that moment thanks to the power of consciousness. Thankfully, the gift of consciousness also gives us the power to see through the illusion of what we think and to go back to the blank page to see what's next.

No matter how long we've let a behaviour define us, no matter how long we've been stuck in a habit of thought, no matter how long we've felt trapped in a feeling, it only takes one thought, one moment of clarity, for that to change. At any time we can have an insight into our human experience that allows us to see our thoughts as sparks of energy and feel no need to fuel the fire. Fires, like thoughts, are naturally self-extinguishing.

Energy is always just changing forms in the universe. It's true in the physical world and true in the psychological world. Without adding fuel, a deserted fire goes from a raging blaze to a few dying embers. Our unhelpful thinking can too.

HERE, THERE & EVERYWHERE

"No problem can be solved from the same level of consciousness that created it." - Albert Einstein

What's beautiful about looking to the unknown for answers is that there's a certain freshness that comes with new thought. One of the reasons it doesn't look obvious to us that our thinking is always changing is because we all have habitual thinking, thoughts we're so accustomed to going with because we've always believed them to be accurate and true.

Habitual thought, as thought, still comes and goes. But if we misunderstand them as reality they tend to take up a lot of mental bandwidth. We naturally give them more energy and attention because they look like a solid feature of life. While we may recognize that new thinking is needed for a solution, if we're so focused on what we've always thought there's very little room for something new to come through.

When we look to the unknown we're looking to the source of where new thought originates. It's the fertile void out of which arises those 'out of the blue' thoughts, that fresh thinking that makes things look completely different than they did just five minutes ago. Every transformation that we've ever had has come from thinking something we've never thought before. It's what changes what we see when we look out through our eyes at our lives. Everything seems different even though nothing on the outside has changed.

When we want new, different, fresh, we have to look to where new, different and fresh comes from. The answers that we seek are not going to come from what we already know — what is already formed — they're going to come from the formless space that is the source of everything. Whether we call it wisdom, common sense, insight, eureka moments, the missing piece, the solution, the answer, however we describe it, there's no getting around the fact that it came from the unknown into the known.

The source of everything can be none other than the pure potential of the universe. Getting a feel for where solutions come from opens us up to seeing more solutions and tends to prevent us from spinning our wheels in old thinking. There are no barriers to entry blocking our access to this deeper mind. We don't have to do anything to earn it or access it, it's provided as our birthright.

Just like a flash of lightning appears from a dark sky out of nowhere, completely unpredictably, a flash of new thought can come into our minds from out of nowhere. We didn't see it before, now we do. This is what it is to have an insight — literally sight from within — that brings a new reality to us. Love, wisdom, clarity, and creativity are often brought to us as insights. They tend to come with a feeling of peace and knowing and change things in our lives seemingly effortlessly. We get a glimpse of a bigger perspective, a higher level of consciousness and it changes our reality.

The same way that lightning strikes as a result of the interplay of natural forces, insight also results from natural forces, the interplay of the three principles of mind, consciousness and thought. We can't know what will occur when, but we know eventually something will because that's how the system is designed.

It's not something we can produce on demand yet it can happen anytime, anywhere. Humans are wired for insight. Every revolutionary scientific or mathematical theory, every great invention, every artistic masterpiece, every stunning piece of music, it all originated in the formless until suddenly it was in form. We are all just skies until lightning strikes.

That's actually how this book came to be. I was showering one winter night minding my own business and suddenly the idea hit me like a strike of lightning. The idea for thematic sections of the four elements comprised of nature metaphors pointing to the essence of the principles seemed to just download into my mind. It was crystal clear, it was completely surprising and it felt like an idea wanting to come through me into the world of form. Following that inspiration is what led to these words on this page. It is both magical and completely ordinary.

Both insight and lightning have the power to illuminate the darkest of moments; everything was dark until suddenly we see the light. It looked like there was no solution until we see it clear as day. Einstein had it right when he saw how a higher level of consciousness is where solutions lie. Understanding that there are deeper levels of wisdom that we can access gives us hope that no matter how solid something looks, it can look completely different in the next moment.

There is an innate capacity we all share: the power to have our minds change. The possibilities for our lives, our relationships, our communities and our world are infinite. We just have to be willing to not know, to stop searching the known for the answers and be open to seeing something new. In a flash, we'll see the light.

A GREAT DAY FOR FREEDOM

"Our species needs, and deserves, a citizenry with minds wide awake and a basic understanding of how the world works." - Carl Sagan

When I first studied Plato's Allegory of the Cave at age sixteen I fell in love with it though I never fully understood it on the level I do now. In brief, the philosopher asks us to consider a scenario in which people have lived their entire life in a dark cave with their necks chained so that all they can see is a cave wall. Behind them lies a fire and any object that passes by that firelight casts shadows on the wall directly in front of them.

If they were to grow up their entire lives believing that shadows are actual objects in the world, they would literally be living in a new world when they discovered what objects truly are and that shadows are a by-product of objects and light. Shadows are simply the resulting phenomena; the natural consequence of an object blocking the light. This allegory has always been fascinating to me philosophically, but it wasn't until I glimpsed that all feelings are the ‘shadows’ of thought that this allegory took on new meaning for me.

We live in the feeling of our thinking. The cause of every feeling we’ve ever had is thought in the moment. It has never, will never, and can never come from causes outside of ourselves. But because it looks really convincing that our experience works outside in, we keep perpetuating the myth that our feelings come from external circumstances. Because this isn't true it tends to get us into a lot of trouble. Our feelings don't come from what our partner said, the driver that cut us off, the number on the scale, our relationship status, our skin colour, upsetting events, or tough situations but rather they come from our thinking about all of those things.

Thought and feeling are two sides of the same coin. We can never have a feeling without thought, even when we aren’t aware of the thought. We can’t feel anything without thought being brought to life by consciousness. That’s just how the system works, the thought-feeling connection is as unbreakable as the light-object-shadow connection. Feelings only come from thought and shadows only come from blocked light.

We culturally believe that we can ‘catch’ bad feelings from people, places and things. When we think the bad feeling is in that situation, independent of how we’re thinking about it, we're doing the mental equivalent of treating the shadow as the object instead of seeing the truth that the shadow is a result of something else. Fortunately what’s true about thought is true of our feelings as well.

When we believe we're getting anxiety from a situation, the onus is on us to change that situation so that we don't feel the accompanying anxiety. But when we see that feeling anxious is 100% caused by having anxious thinking in the moment, suddenly it doesn’t make sense to spend our time and effort trying to change the situation. When we see the thought-feeling connection we can wake up to the true source of where our experience comes from, with all its fluidity, variance and flow. We can wait for the next thought-feeling to arise within us, as it naturally will, without a single thing in the outside world needing to change.

Because I misunderstood where my anxious feelings were coming from I was set on eliminating "anxiety-provoking" situations from my life. So I would avoid certain people, places and things only to discover that I still felt anxious! I didn't see that it was coming from me, independent of what was happening externally, and so my "solution" never solved anything. Knowing that my anxious feelings were a result of anxious thinking and that anxious thinking was just a normal part of human life that meant nothing about me or my life, I was able to stop holding on to that experience and let something new show up.

Instead of being terrified by the shadows because we mistake them for solid real world objects that can get us, which is essentially what the prisoners in the cave concluded, we can start to realize a deeper truth. They aren't coming from the externals in our life, nor are they permanent. They are psychological shadows, the natural consequence of a temporary thought-form.

No matter how scary a shadow looks, regardless of its shape, size or duration, it's still just the natural consequence of an object blocking some light. Consciousness is like the illuminated cave wall, mind is the energy behind the light, and thought is just the form that happens to be moving through the light of consciousness in any given moment.

The resulting shadow is simply a feeling: it only exists as long as the object is there, it disappears as soon as the object leaves. Unlike the cave, thought isn't even an object, it's simply an energy. Feelings are simply energetic shadows, there until they're no longer there, and there's so much freedom to be found in that.

EARTH

HERE COMES THE SUN

"Look deep into nature, and then you will understand everything better." - *Albert Einstein*

Nature has a natural cycle to it. The planets rotate and orbit in a predictable manner. The moon causes tides to rise and fall everyday. The earth flows into four seasons a year based on a location's relation to the sun. Everyday we have day and night. Some days are windy, some calm. Some days are sunny, others cloudy. Weather, whether on a seasonal scale or daily scale, cycles naturally as a result of pre-existing forces.

When I learned about the principles behind the human experience I realized that we all work the same way. Regardless of circumstance human beings will cycle into high and low moods. Regardless of background we all have great moments and bad moments. Regardless of our age or life experience, we'll see some things with more clarity than others.

Bit by bit I realized I could trust the cycles of nature to keep moving and changing even when what I was looking at seemed to not change. Just because I wasn't seeing something in the moment didn't mean there was nothing there to see. I realized that a low mood didn't mean that something in my life needed fixing. It simply meant that I was having a completely safe, temporary human experience. One experience would flow into the next experience without my doing. That's just how the system works.

This took so much pressure off needing to figure out the perfect formula in order to feel good more often. Before I understood that the variance of experience is inevitable, I believed that it was up to me to control my experience of life and have things be just right.

So when my mood dropped and I was lost in the darkness, I took that as a sign that action was needed in my life. I spun my wheels thinking about how I could change my circumstances so that I would feel differently. I didn't know that if I left my thinking alone, I would feel better naturally. I never knew the system was self-correcting.

No one told me if I just let my experience be I would have a new one without having to do anything! I wish somebody had told me that my doing, striving, and analyzing were only getting in the way of the fresh thinking, peace of mind and insight that were trying to bubble up.

When I didn't know this the dark times felt really dark. It felt like what I would imagine our ancestors felt when they weren't sure if the sun would to rise in the morning. I'm sure at some point they either figured the darkness would be eternal or that rituals and sacrifices were needed to bring back the sun.

Once I saw that my mood had its own natural cycle I was free to let my mood rise and fall without thinking it was a problem. Every time the sun appears to set, I know there will be a sun rise. Every time my mood drops, I know my mood will rise. I have faith that the system will continue to operate the way it always has in the past. I no longer fear that the darkness will be permanent.

Every time my level of consciousness dips, I know eventually it will go back up, no rituals or sacrifices needed. My mood could lift while on a walk, in the bathtub, on the phone with a friend, or while eating but I know none of those actions cause my mood to change. It rises and falls on its own accord. I don't have to concern myself with the how or why.

The freedom in knowing this has completely changed my relationship to bad moods. It has completely changed my relationship to anxious thinking. The beauty of understanding anything, especially these principles, is that when we understand the nature of something we wake up to how predictably it works. This takes the fear out of it. It is freeing to see how unchanging principles are.

Knowing that it has always worked a particular way and always will gives us a sense of comfort. Even when it looks and feels as though the darkness is everlasting, it will eventually end. Daylight will come, no rituals or superstitions needed. The sun will rise because that's what the sun does. It doesn't get any simpler than that.

TRUTH IS A BEAUTIFUL THING

"The things best to know are first principles and causes, but these things are perhaps the most difficult for men to grasp, for they are farthest removed from the senses." - Aristotle

When the world encounters a new paradigm it literally changes our worldview from the ground up. Its implications extend far beyond the immediate facts of the new paradigm, it forms a new foundation on which other things rest on.

One notable paradigm shift that changed the course of history dramatically was the adoption of a heliocentric solar system as opposed to a geocentric solar system. Another was the discovery that germs, microorganisms invisible to the naked eye, were responsible for deaths and illnesses previously blamed on noxious air. And of course there was even a time when the prevailing paradigm was that the earth was flat. Previous to the realization that the earth had no edges, oceanic explorers would have to continuously keep a lookout for the end of the earth so that they didn't accidentally fall off into space.

Sure, this may sound ridiculous, but that's because now that we see truth it's hard to believe that we ever believed and acted on false assumptions. That's the beauty of a paradigm shift, once we discover and reconnect with truth, we see the ridiculousness, futility and overall unhelpfulness of living life as if something is true when it's not.

For the world to see the truth of these psychological principles would shift the psychological paradigm from outside-in to inside-out. Whenever we manage to understand the foundational facts of how we all actually operate, the implications and applications built from that foundation are naturally helpful. They're effective because they are aligned with truth; it's a bottom-up process. If the very foundation is incorrect, it affects everything built on that mistake.

Needing constant surveillance for the edge of the earth doesn't make sense if the earth doesn't have edges. Until the heliocentric paradigm was accepted the math wasn't adding up, celestial bodies didn't behave as predicted. Scientists were scrambling to identify hidden causes of why the physics were skewed because they didn't see that the fundamental assumption that the earth is the centre of the universe was the cause of their errors.

When I look around at the state of the world today, in 2018, it's so obvious to me that the world's problems, whether cultural, social, economic, political, environmental, biological, physical, psychological or emotional are the logical consequences of living life with a fundamental misunderstanding about the nature of the human experience. In a world where we're collectively conditioned to believe that our experience is coming from outside us, from people, places, things, titles, status, and more, it makes a lot of sense why we're seeing the problems of today. When one engineers a bridge with faulty physics, it's going to collapse.

When we fail to see that actually the sun is the centre of our solar system, the scientific calculations of celestial distances are going to be incorrect. When we fail to see what truly makes us feel good when we feel good, and feel bad when we feel bad, we'll praise and blame all the wrong things. That's just the nature of paradigms; it's what happens when false assumptions are taken as truth. If it really looks like our well-being is dependent on outside circumstances, we'll dismiss the moments when we feel good without them, and overestimate how much better our lives will be once we've achieved our goals.

The good news is that when the fundamental mistake is cleared up, the practical, reasonable and logical next steps become much more obvious. Given that germs exists, surgeons should be as sterile as possible to reduce the risk of transmission. Given that planets rotate around the sun, we can predict moon cycles and tidal patterns. Given that our experience is always generated from the three principles of mind, consciousness and thought, it stands to reason that we all live in separate realities, we feel our thinking as though it's true, and there's a larger intelligence constantly refreshing our human experience.

Correct the underlying assumptions and what derives from that will be infinitely more helpful. Regardless of the desired end result, getting the physics right is crucial for any bit of engineering. Almost all of our actions are based on the false assumptions we have about the source of our happiness or suffering. Once that's corrected the rest becomes obvious.

GRAVITY

"Reality is merely an illusion, albeit a very persistent one."
- Albert Einstein

Gaining an understanding of the principles is not about belief. What I mean is that whether or not somebody believes the principles to be true, it doesn't change the fact that the principles are working perfectly in them every moment they're alive. Anyone can claim that they don't believe that experience works inside-out and yet I can see that the inside-out nature of experience is what is allowing them to have that thought.

Because these principles are fundamental truths, they work regardless of belief. The same way that gravity is a fundamental principle of the physical world, mind, thought and consciousness are the fundamental principles of how all humans come to experience life. As principles, they are not concerned with whether we believe them or not. Someone can make it their life's work to disbelieve gravity and yet when they trip on a sidewalk they will fall towards the ground every single time. Even if they don’t believe it, even if they don’t remember how gravity works. People who don’t believe in gravity don’t simply float away. Gravity does not care what ideas someone makes up about it.

Gravity is completely unaffected by whether or not we notice it happening; it is a force that works regardless of our belief about it. It has been working before we got here and will continue working after we go. Principles are incredibly predictable and when something is predictable it's less frightening. We don’t have to worry that every fifth time we trip we’ll go flying off into space. I know if I lose my balance I’ll consistently fall towards the earth every single time.

Likewise, understanding the inside-out nature of our experience means we’ll always know what direction to look. We’ll certainly feel different thoughts, feelings and realities throughout life but it's always the principles, not events, people or situations, behind that experience. That means we're never stuck in anything, we're always free to have a different experience because that's built-in to the design.

Sydney Banks did not invent human experience arising from formless spiritual principles. Humans don't have the power to invent natural laws. They may only uncover, and do their best to describe, these formless forces. Syd had a moment of enlightenment in which he glimpsed the very fabric of reality and did his best to put words around that realization, yet the principles have always been here.

One of the things that’s so powerful about understanding pre-existing forces is that we see the impersonal nature of it; it’s not about us, it never was. We know that when we drop our favourite mug and it breaks, it wasn't because gravity was out to get us. When we fall on the ice it's not because gravity decided in that moment to work for us or against us, as bodies with mass we're simply subject to the pre-existing forces in the universe.

When I began to see that the principles were impersonal forces suddenly I didn't have to put so much weight on the specific experiences that were arising within me. I didn't care so much what showed up, I still had personal preferences of course but I didn't need to take anger, anxiety, sadness or judgment about myself or others as seriously.

Just like physical falls, I didn't have to take my emotional falls personally. I didn't have to be a victim of my experience. When I was seeing clearly, I really saw that it was not personal. This in turn has helped me see that when others are in low moods they're simply believing in the illusion of their thinking and feeling disconnected. How they're seeing life in that moment is just that: how they're seeing life. It is not a reflection of them as a person.

Imagine a world where when people did harmful things it was understood that those actions only made sense from a place of insecure thought and a low level of consciousness. Imagine if we saw that it wasn't a personal failing, it was simply the result of falling for the illusion that what we think is true which stems from misunderstanding. How compassionate would we all be with each other if we could see that we're all up against the same thing. How different would it be if we helped those struggling and suffering instead of locking them up and vilifying them.

I used to always take what others did personally. I used to think what they did was about me. Now that I know what they're feeling is being brought to life within them through the power of mind, thought and consciousness, I know that what they do is not about them either.

We all live in separate realities, once we recognize that fact we don't have to take our own or anyone else's reality too seriously.

From time to time we all just innocently misunderstand where our experience comes from. It comes from whatever form the energy of thought takes in the moment, made real by consciousness and powered by a universal intelligence that is continually recreating our reality. This occurs regardless of whether or not I believe it. Regardless of whether or not you believe it. Regardless of whether it appears that way or not. We can absolutely make how we're feeling about us, take it personally, and identify with it, or we can look towards the impersonal nature, see that it's truly not about us and let it flow through as easily and naturally as it was designed.

GROW BIG, GROW BEAUTIFUL

"Here is my secret, a very simple secret: It is only with the heart that one can see rightly; what is essential is invisible to the eye."
- Antoine de Saint-Exupery

The principle of mind, the intelligent energy that powers life, is difficult to describe. It's not easy to put words around the energy that is the source of everything in the universe. It is the great nothingness, the all-that-is, the pure energy that creates and operates everything in existence.

It's the energy that grows seeds into trees. Even though a seed does not look alive at first glance, if we place it in soil with some water and some sunlight it will begin to sprout. It then grows, develops stems and leaves, starts the automatic process of converting sunlight into usable energy, grows bigger and taller, exchanges nutrients with the environment, exchanges gases with the air, and eventually becomes this majestic beautiful tree that can live for centuries.

That is mind in action. We can see it in everything because it's the source of absolutely everything. It's how salmon know to return to spawn in the stream they were born. It's how birds know how to fly in aerodynamic formations and migrate south for the winter. It's how predators know how to catch their prey, and prey know how to escape their predators. It's behind evolution, instincts and all those things we just know without being taught. It's spinning the planets, manifesting weather, and infusing the life force into all living creatures. It's what is beating our hearts, breathing our lungs and creating our experience of life.

I wasn't always aware our minds are built to replenish. I didn't know renewal was built-in to the human system. I didn't always see that the mind naturally heals from unpleasant experiences. I had no idea that the mind would bring more healthy, useful thinking once I stopped diving into the content of my current thinking.

In hindsight it makes so much sense. Of course we wouldn't have bodies that are self-healing but have minds that we have to heal ourselves. When our skin gets cut, the intelligence behind life heals it. When an object gets too close to our eyes, we automatically blink. When we touch something too hot or cold we quickly pull our hand away. When we come into contact with viruses we have a whole immune system designed to raise our defences and keep us healthy. We naturally fall asleep because our bodies produce a daily hormonal shift that lulls us to rest.

Our minds are designed with the same self-correcting mechanisms as our bodies. Because we've misunderstood the source of our human experience we've innocently created a world that is out of alignment with how life works. We don't need to heal ourselves. We just need to get out of the way and let healing happen naturally. Interfering with the healing process by employing tools and techniques stops making sense when we see that we're innocently getting in our own way. We only engage in counterproductive behaviours because they make sense in that moment given how reality looks to us. Change is effortless once we see how little there is for us to do.

The same energy that grows trees out of seeds and heals us physically can bring us solutions to any problem, show us the big picture and root us in our connection to everything in the universe. There is nothing this universal energy isn't capable of. It is pure potential, flowing through everything in existence. It can do life better than we can. All we need to do is look to what this source is already doing for us, and see that we don't need to do nearly as much as we think.

THE SONG REMAINS THE SAME

"Everyone is doing the best they can, given the thinking that looks real to them." - Sydney Banks

So much in the world of form appears more separate than it truly is; we don't always see the inherent connection in things that seem so different. Getting a sense that fundamentally all experience works the same is something I find really hopeful, especially when we're struggling with things that feel extremely difficult or very personal.

I used to think, like so much of our culture seems to believe, that the solution to mental distress came from sorting out the details. I thought there was very different root causes for mental distress depending on the manifestation of the symptoms. I paid lots of attention to the details, thinking they were the relevant bit, the key that would unlock freedom.

This understanding has allowed me to see past the specific details of how psychological experience is manifesting in the moment to glimpse the bigger picture of what's occurring in all instances of psychological distress. It looks to me now that anytime someone is suffering mentally it's due to the fact that they're having an experience of thought that looks and feels so real they mistake it for an experience of reality. It's an ephemeral energy appearing as objective, solid fact. It's always the same thing happening: we innocently take our thinking as truth and suffer as a result.

It looks to me that any and all mental distress, and dare I say mental illness, is rooted in a misunderstanding about our experience: where it comes from, what it is, how it operates, what it means and what we need to do about it. Correct this misunderstanding and our innate health rises to the surface. We become reconnected to who we truly are simply because we've seen through the interference covering it up.

Having seen so many of my own unhelpful habits, labels and diagnoses fall away over time as I looked in this direction, it's easy to see that my psychological suffering was kept alive through misunderstanding. I was doing the best I could do at the time, I honestly truly was. I know everyone else is doing the best they can too. Faulty information will lead to faulty conclusions, no matter how hard someone is trying.

On the surface it appeared as though my anxiety, depression, habits, obsessive-compulsive tendencies and insecurities were separate problems with separate root causes. In truth they're all symptoms of the same problem. Reflecting on this made me realize that looking and feeling different does not mean it's not the same at its core.

Take wood, for example. Wood can be found as bark on living trees, in piles of sawdust, as paper, as a splinter, as painted baseboards in our house, as a steering wheel on a boat, as a deck, as furniture, as doors, as shoes, as a log cabin and in countless other forms. Fundamentally, no matter the form or context, it's still made of wood.

No matter how our psychological suffering is labelled, whether as depression, a low mood, a horrible thought, anxiety, nightmares, panic attacks, stress, etc, it still comes down to thought being taken as reality. It comes down to a temporary manifestation of universal energy being taken as an unshakable truth about life or about us. The great news for all seven billion of us, is even though it looks that way, it's simply not true.

I once heard George Pransky talk about how no matter what type of thoughts are going through our minds, if we have enough perspective to see them as just thoughts brought to life in the moment instead of as an objective reality, we have reconnected with our innate mental health. It does not matter what the thoughts are or what they are about, our mental health is a reflection of our relationship to our thinking.

Whether it be delusions, panic, or violent murderous thoughts, as long as we can see that it is coming from thought in the moment and not from reality, we naturally won't be inclined to take that thinking as seriously, and it'll keep on flowing through us as it was designed to do.

DAZED AND CONFUSED

Whenever we're in a low mood we don't see life clearly. A low mood, with all its icky feelings, tells us in that moment we've lost access to our perspective and clarity. How life looks in that moment is very biased, subjective and personal. Things look more urgent, people look more problematic, circumstances look more dire and overall we tend to feel hopeless. Luckily this is telling us we're at a low level of consciousness; feelings are our internal warning signals.

For simplicity's sake we can think of it as being in our right mind or not in our right mind. When we're in our right mind, we can trust the decisions and actions that come from that place. They'll tend to be more loving, wise and cooperative. When we're not in our right mind, we simply have to wait until we're in our right mind once again. Because the mind is self-correcting we won't be stuck in our low mood forever, our mood will rise and we'll see clearly again.

When we make decisions from a low mood we risk taking actions that would never make sense to do when we feel good. When our minds are very full, busy and revved up, our clarity and wisdom takes a backseat to the noise in our head. All bad habits start out as actions taken when we weren't feeling like ourselves and wanted to feel better. We naturally strive to go back to our default state of well-being and we'll often take our brain's suggestions on how best to do that. The quick fixes we try may have undesirable consequences, but they're truly our best attempt to feel better in the moment.

If we want to make better choices, live with less regrets, and hurt others less it's incredibly beneficial to see that we don't have to take our low mood thinking seriously. We don't have to act on any of that thinking. The very fact that it's low mood thinking means it's unreliable, untrustworthy and shouldn't be taken seriously. It's too subjective, biased, and personal to be useful to navigate our lives.

It would be like driving in a snowstorm. When there are blizzard conditions, black ice, freezing rain, howling winds and slush, it's best to stay inside and wait for the storm to pass. It's not a good idea to try to drive somewhere in it, the risk of danger is too high. Yet we often innocently take low mood thinking as a sign that we need to fix something in our lives. If we don't see it for what it is (thought in the moment that arises independently of the world of form) we're likely to act in a way that's counter-productive. We'll make decisions, have conversations and take action from a place where our wisdom and clarity is obscured by a lot of thought.

Whenever we're caught up in our heads and life looks bleak we've temporarily lost touch with our inherent wisdom and common sense that's able to guide us through life. And so, just like driving in a snowstorm, we're going out in life with low visibility. It's not to say that we can't drive in the snowstorm, many of us head out in real and metaphorical snowstorms all the time. It's just worth noticing that it's much easier for us to get stuck, lose our bearings, lose our sense of direction and do harm to ourselves and others when we aren't seeing clearly.

On a bright, clear, dry, sunny day everything looks different. Suddenly we regain our visibility, can see the big picture and are able to get traction. Getting where we want to go is a lot easier, quicker and safer. The reason this is important is two-fold. Firstly being in a low mood, at a lower level of consciousness, is when things feel the most urgent, gripping, and real. In that state of mind it feels more than ever like we need to take action to get somewhere other than here.

This is why the worst time for a couple to bring up an issue is when they're already arguing. In that state of mind neither of them is seeing clearly. Neither of them are in touch with their inherent capabilities of problem-solving, compassion, love and understanding. When their minds self-correct they'll gain perspective and the solutions will be obvious. As much as it looks like that moment is the time to be fixing problems, when we see it for the thought-storm that it is we can take refuge until the storm naturally clears out.

The second reason this is so important is that literally every tragedy, social issue, or personal mistake has occurred from someone being caught up in their thinking and unaware that what they think isn't true. In that low state of mind they take their perceptions as truth and act from that place. Everything from a terrorist attack, to someone drinking themselves to death, to environmental degradation to racist comments is the result of decisions that were made in the mental equivalent of snowstorm driving. They weren't seeing clearly in the moment but if they'd just allowed the storm to clear out they'd be reunited with their common sense.

Once people see how it works they can allow their minds to clear when they feel off. There's nothing to do but just allow the storm to pass through. In a clear mind they're reunited with their common sense which enables them to make good decisions, have perspective, seek alternatives, get solutions, remain open to possibilities, take actions aligned with their true nature, see the big picture and engage in loving relationships with others. On a sunny day the path is evident, in a snowstorm not so much.

ANY COLOUR YOU LIKE

"All feelings derive and become alive, whether negative or positive, from the power of Thought." - Sydney Banks

What I find incredibly comforting about learning these principles is that we start to see that anything that we're experiencing, no matter how different it looks, no matter how isolating it feels, no matter how awful it sounds, is still just the same universal energy disguised in a temporary form. Elation and anxiety are the same thing in different costumes. Depression and bliss are both forms that this energy can take in our human system.

We're so accustomed to noticing the details that we see the disguises for their differences rather than their similarities. Yet its essence is fundamentally the same. Regardless of how different we feel when we're anxious, depressed or grateful, the system still operates the same way. Consciousness brings all thought to life, not just the ones we like or dislike.

Thought is always changing form, appearing and disappearing, and flowing through our system, whether we judge it as desirable or not. What Syd glimpsed in his moment of enlightenment was that all is one. The energy of mind is the great all-ness, the great oneness. At the same time, it is the great nothingness, the unknown. The yet to be created. It is everything and it is no thing. It is what allows any of us to change in an instant, once we see something new, we will literally be living in a different reality. It was a subjective made-up 'reality' all along, which is what allows it to get created and recreated in any moment.

Our minds are like prisms. Within the pure white light lies every colour of the rainbow. The colours are simply different wavelengths, energy vibrations at different frequencies. The nature of prisms is to refract light, splitting the pure light into a particular wavelength. Universal Mind is the pure white light running through every living thing.

As soon as this universal energy shows up in our system it gets fractionated into different wavelengths, colours of experience, that we then assign meaning to, label, judge, use as evidence, take seriously, believe or otherwise imbue with energy and attention. Sad feelings are like a bit of blue light getting refracted from the prism and brought to life through our consciousness. Then our minds refract a different bit of light, some red colour wavelengths that we recognize as fear. Then some green light comes through the prism and we feel calm.

Of course these colours, and their corresponding emotions, are simply a metaphor, but hopefully it gives a sense of how the same pure energy that powers the entire universe appears in different forms in different moments. It's a never-ending dance. The form of thought gives us a temporary experience in the moment. Each moment is the result of an internally generated movie that we've innocently projected out through our eyeballs.

Thus, our lives look really beautiful, hopeful and magical one day and really scary, difficult and hopeless the next. This is why sometimes I hear of a bombing and freak out, become fearful for the state of the world and decide that I'm taking that country off my bucket list. Yet a week later I can hear of a similar bombing and feel no fear, only a deep sense of compassion for all those affected and wonder how different life would be if only most people understood how the human mind works. The bombings aren't creating my experience, my thinking in the moment is.

If I hear the news when there's blue wavelengths colouring my experience I'll feel one way. If I hear the news while green wavelengths are colouring my experience I'll feel differently. I can go from nervousness to excitement to fear to hope to calm without a single thing in my situation changing. Different thought is the only variable that needs to change for a different experience. It's still the same pure white light flowing through me, I simply have an experience of whatever colour is shining through my consciousness in the moment. The possibility for any experience exists in any moment. It's just a matter of seeing for ourselves that pure light can take many different forms, literally any colour we can imagine.

A computer is said to be able to display around seventeen million different colours when all the variations of tone, hue, and value are accounted for. Similarly, there are as many different experiences of the same event as there are people in the world. No two people will experience the same event in exactly the same way because they'll never have exactly the same thinking about it in the moment. Their experience will be completely unique because it's always and only a reflection of what form the energy of thought takes in that moment. This is what is behind people's ability to handle extraordinarily difficult circumstances with ease and grace. And also why people can have a complete meltdown over one insignificant thing not going their way. One energy, infinite number of forms.

FINAL WORDS

Fortunately I hope you're starting to get the sense that there's less to do than you think. It's not about doing better, it's about seeing more of what's universally true. There is nothing you need to do, nor anything you can do, to make this true. It's true that life has a way of supporting us and carrying us. That there's a constant river of change and renewal. There is a depth of our being that is stillness, untouched by our temporary experience. It's human to have lots of thinking about certain areas of our lives, it's all okay. Feelings move through us in waves, appearing and disappearing from the formless energy behind life.

So much of life is done for us, there's much less to do than we think. We don't see things as they are, we see them as we are. Or said another way, what we think isn't true, it's just what we think. Life is not what it appears to be, we're tricked into an illusion that we can see through at times. Life is a divine dream we treat as reality, our scary thinking is no more real than our nightmares. We are the blue sky, what we experience is simply the weather.

We're constantly powered by the creative force behind life. We don't have to deal with what's already formed, we can let new form show up in any moment. We don't have to pour energy, attention and meaning into our experience. We're wired for insights, fresh ideas, innovation and creativity. We can understand our feelings, and in understanding become more comfortable with feeling uncomfortable. There's a natural ebb and flow to our moods.

Having an accurate view of what's going on changes our relationship to it. Principles are fundamental forces that have no exceptions, they are universal and constant. Our minds are self-correcting by nature. Looking at the details tends to obscure, confuse and separate; underneath the specifics the system works the same in everyone. When we're seeing clearly we have all the answers we need. We're always feeling the creative manifestation of this universal energy in any moment.

Nature is a wonderful teacher because it shows us what we cannot easily see is happening in ourselves. We are all intrinsically powered by universal mind, all living in thought-created realities brought to life by consciousness that look and feel incredibly real. Any moment we can ever have is a function of these three principles working within us to create our experience of life. Principles are not nice ideas, they are the fundamental truths behind how the human system works.

We are all built with a default state of wisdom, love and well-being that exists completely independent of the circumstances we're in, the experiences we're having or the decisions we're making. We are intrinsically connected to the grandest, most intelligent force in the universe. Being open to seeing our own insights into these facts leads to transformation and the rediscovery of our innate health. We are alive, we are aware and we think. So simple, yet powerful in its implications. As Syd loved to remind people "we're only one thought away".

GRATITUDE

I don't take any credit as the source of all the metaphors in this book. I tried to sort which ones seemed to randomly appear in my mind and which ones I've heard before from who, when, and in what context, but they've been used in this conversation so frequently and with so much variance that I found it impossible to accurately track. I owe so much praise and gratitude to my lovely teachers and mentors in this understanding and to the originators I am deeply grateful.

How do I even begin to express my deep love and gratitude for all the incredible teachers who pointed me towards these truths. Dr Amy Johnson you were the first person to turn my world inside out, you changed my life and I'm eternally grateful.

Dr Dicken Bettinger, Dr Bill Pettit, Dr Mark Howard, Mara Gleason Olsen, Eirik Grunde Olsen, Cathy Casey, Elsie Spittle, Dr Aaron Turner, Dr George Pransky, Linda Pransky, Erika Bugbee, Kara Stamback, and Michael Neill the direction you've pointed me towards has been invaluable in seeing these truths deeper for myself. Thank you for all the amazing work you do, humanity is beyond blessed to have you.

My beautiful friends and family, thank you for your unwavering love and support. I could not have done it without you. So grateful for my beta readers for taking the time to make this book the best it could be: Mindy Sonshine, Antra Boyd, Julia Heinz, Michelle Coish and Lindsey Reed, you guys are rock stars.

Last but not least, thank you Sydney Banks for having the courage to share your insights with the world. Your contribution to the world is immeasurable; you've led us all back home.

RECOMMENDED READING

Fortunately there are so many other amazing books sharing these principles, listed below are just some of my favourites, the ones I come back to time and time again...

Sydney Banks' *The Missing Link*

Sydney Banks' *The Enlightened Gardener*

Sydney Banks' *The Enlightened Gardener Revisisted*

Mara Gleason's *One Thought Changes Everything*

Michael Neill's *The Inside-Out Revolution*

Dr Amy Johnson's *The Little Book of Big Change*

Dr George Pransky's *The Relationship Handbook*

Dr. Dicken Bettinger & Natasha Swerdloff's *Coming Home*

ABOUT THE AUTHOR

Shannon Cooper is a transformative coach and author living in beautiful Rossland, British Columbia, Canada. Having graduated from the University of Victoria with a degree in philosophy and environmental studies, her passion is sparking more wisdom, well-being and peace in the world. To learn more and stay in the conversation connect with her at evergreeninsight.com

29647016R00058

Printed in Great Britain
by Amazon